SUPER TRUCKS

Series Creator:

David Salariya was born in Dundee, Scotland, where he studied illustration and printmaking. He has illustrated a wide range of books and has created many new series of books for publishers in the UK and overseas. In 1989 he established The Salariya Book Company. He lives in Brighton with his wife, the illustrator Shirley Willis, and their son Jonathan.

Artist:

Nick Hewetson was educated in Sussex at Brighton Technical School and studied illustration at Eastbourne College of Art. He has since illustrated a wide variety of children's books.

Artist:

Mark Bergin was born in Hastings in 1961. He studied at Eastbourne College of Art and has specialised in historical reconstructions, aviation and maritime subjects since 1983. He has been commissioned by aerospace companies and has illustrated a number of books on flight. He has illustrated many books in the prize-winning *Inside Story* series as well as **Space Shuttle**, **Wonders of the World** and **Castle** in the *Fast Forward* series.

Author:

Ian Graham was born in Belfast in 1953. He studied applied physics at The City University, London, and took a postgraduate diploma in journalism at the same university, specialising in science and technology journalism. After four years as an editor of consumer electronics magazines, he became a freelance author and journalist. Since then, he has written more than one hundred children's non-fiction books and numerous magazine articles.

Editor:

Karen Barker Smith

Editorial Assistant:

Stephanie Cole

Created, designed and produced by
THE SALARIYA BOOK COMPANY LTD
25 Marlborough Place, Brighton BN1 1UB

Published in Great Britain in 2001 by
Hodder Wayland, an imprint of
Hodder Children's Books

A Catalogue record for this book is available from the British Library.

ISBN 0 7502 3628 0

Printed in Hong Kong

Hodder Children's Books
A division of Hodder Headline Ltd
338 Euston Road, London NW1 3BH

SUPER TRUCKS

Written by
IAN GRAHAM

Illustrated by
MARK BERGIN
and
NICK HEWETSON

Created and designed by
DAVID SALARIYA

W
HODDER
Wayland

An imprint of Hodder Children's Books

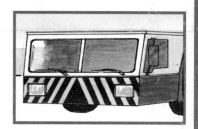

Contents

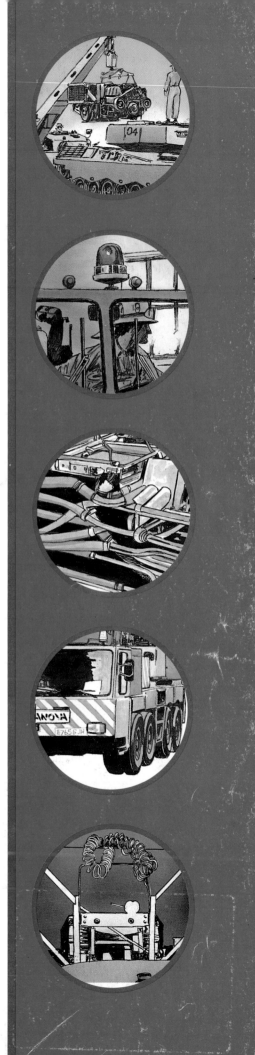

The First Trucks

1898 Daimler

The first self-propelled trucks were steam-powered monsters. They were heavy and slow with engines that belched black smoke. Before they could start, the driver had to light the boiler and heat a tank of water to get up a head of steam. Motor trucks, which were first produced in Germany in the 1890s, were a great improvement. They were ready to go as soon as their petrol engines were started. However, most freight was still hauled by horse-drawn wagons and steam locomotives until trucks proved their usefulness during World War I (1914-18). The thousands of military trucks left over after the war started a new road haulage industry in Europe and the USA in the 1920s. Manufacturers started making new vehicles specially designed to carry freight. Driver comfort was not a high priority in these early trucks. The cab was often open to the weather and solid rubber tyres gave a bumpy, uncomfortable ride.

The German engineer Gottlieb Daimler built the first motor truck in 1896. It had a four horsepower engine. Like the 1898 model shown above, it was little more than a motorised platform with a seat, but it was the latest thing in truck technology at the time.

Autocar 2 Tons

The Autocar 2 Tons (left) was introduced in 1926. Early models had an open cab, with only a short roof to cover the driver. '2 Tons' referred to the weight the truck could carry. The truck itself weighed 7-10 tonnes, depending on the model – there were 20 versions. Autocar is one of the oldest US truck manufacturers. It began in 1897 as the Pittsburgh Motor Car Company.

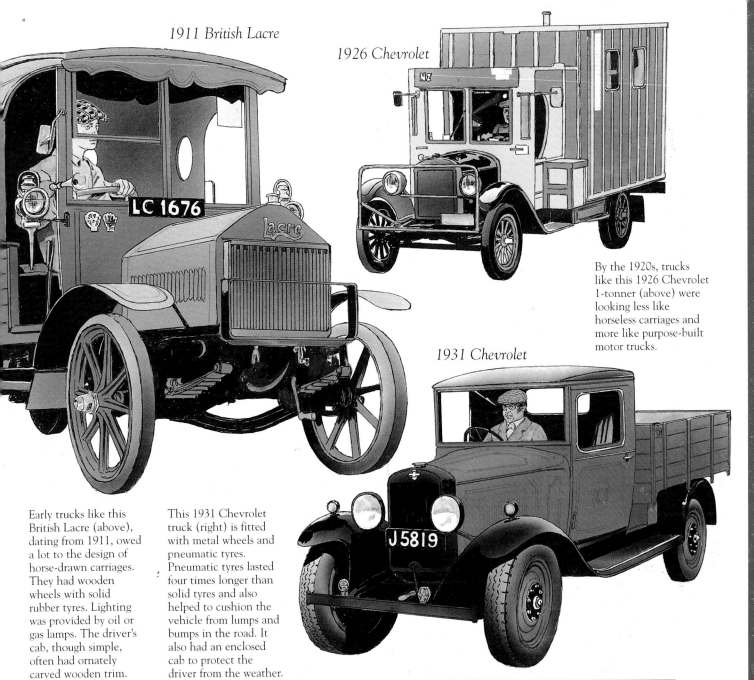

1911 British Lacre

1926 Chevrolet

LC 1676

Lacre

By the 1920s, trucks like this 1926 Chevrolet 1-tonner (above) were looking less like horseless carriages and more like purpose-built motor trucks.

1931 Chevrolet

J 5819

Early trucks like this British Lacre (above), dating from 1911, owed a lot to the design of horse-drawn carriages. They had wooden wheels with solid rubber tyres. Lighting was provided by oil or gas lamps. The driver's cab, though simple, often had ornately carved wooden trim.

This 1931 Chevrolet truck (right) is fitted with metal wheels and pneumatic tyres. Pneumatic tyres lasted four times longer than solid tyres and also helped to cushion the vehicle from lumps and bumps in the road. It also had an enclosed cab to protect the driver from the weather.

Early trucks spent much more time off the road than modern vehicles, because they had to be loaded and unloaded by hand.

Trucks for Tasks

Trucks are vehicles used to carry freight by road. The shape and size of every truck is decided according to the task it is intended for. The design begins with the chassis, the main frame on which the rest of the truck is built. The chassis is made from steel beams welded into the shape of a ladder running the length of the truck. Some of the smallest trucks, or vans, are no bigger than cars and use the same type of petrol engine as cars. Most trucks are powered by diesel engines because they are simpler, stronger, more reliable and less expensive to operate than petrol engines. The number of wheels a truck has depends on the weight it will have to carry. Heavier trucks need more wheels to spread their weight evenly over the road. Some types of trucks are equipped with machinery, such as a winch, to pull things on-board or a hoist to lift things on and off. Most trucks are able to carry a variety of different sorts of freight, but some trucks are specialised to do one particular task. Trucks designed for special tasks include fire engines, military transporters, concrete trucks, refrigerated food transporters, tow trucks and road cranes.

Some recovery trucks have a rear platform that tilts down to the ground (right). A car can then be winched up onto the platform, which tips up level again. Like tow trucks, these recovery vehicles are used to collect broken-down cars and to remove illegally parked or abandoned vehicles.

Tankers transport all sorts of liquids. They deliver petrol to fuel stations and a variety of liquid chemicals to manufacturers.

Trucks can haul even larger loads by towing trailers behind them. A truck-plus-trailer is called a drawbar-trailer outfit.

Wreckers, or tow trucks, collect vehicles that have broken down or have been involved in accidents. They tow them away by using a winch mounted on the rear of the vehicle.

Winch

Airport tugs or tractors are strange-looking vehicles used to move aircraft. Most of the vehicle is taken up by its powerful diesel engine, with a small driver's cab at the front. Tugs are built very low and flat so that they can fit underneath an airliner's nose and hook up to its nose wheel to tow it.

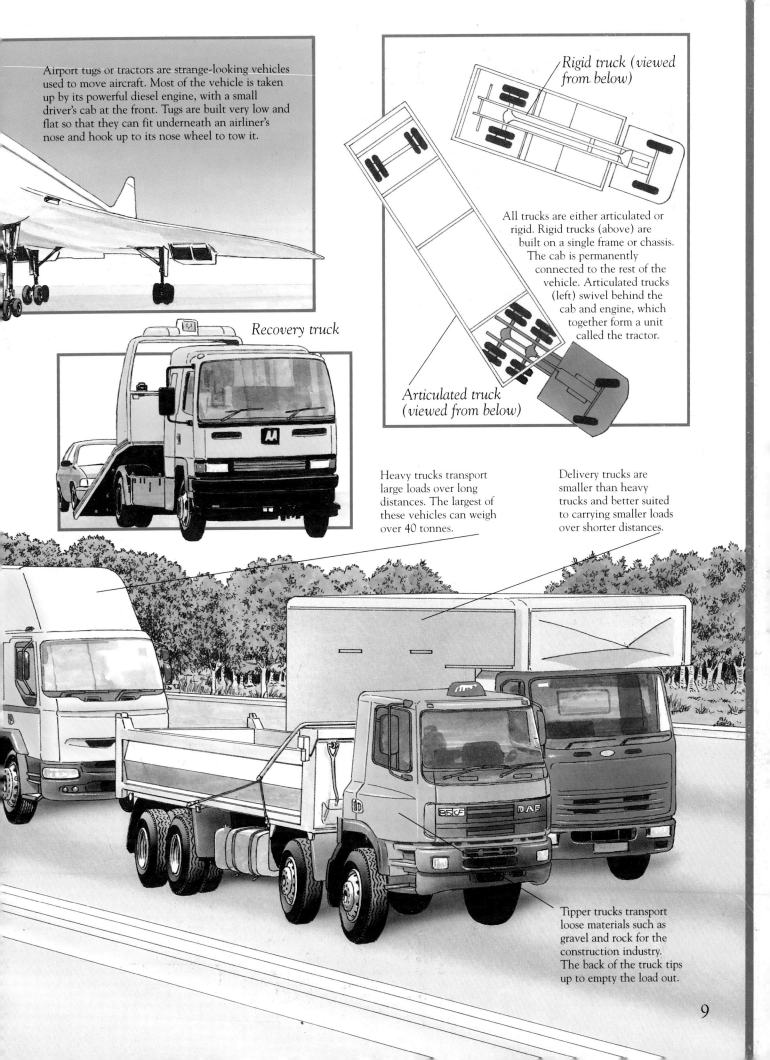

Rigid truck (viewed from below)

All trucks are either articulated or rigid. Rigid trucks (above) are built on a single frame or chassis. The cab is permanently connected to the rest of the vehicle. Articulated trucks (left) swivel behind the cab and engine, which together form a unit called the tractor.

Articulated truck (viewed from below)

Recovery truck

Heavy trucks transport large loads over long distances. The largest of these vehicles can weigh over 40 tonnes.

Delivery trucks are smaller than heavy trucks and better suited to carrying smaller loads over shorter distances.

Tipper trucks transport loose materials such as gravel and rock for the construction industry. The back of the truck tips up to empty the load out.

9

Truck Racing

Trucks are the most unlikely racing vehicles. They are designed to carry equipment, make deliveries or haul heavy loads, not to race. However, truck racing is very popular. All sorts of trucks are raced, from open-back pick-up trucks to articulated truck tractor units. Today's racing trucks are specially built, with racing engines designed and tuned for high-speed manoeuvring on the track. These make racing trucks as powerful as many racing cars.

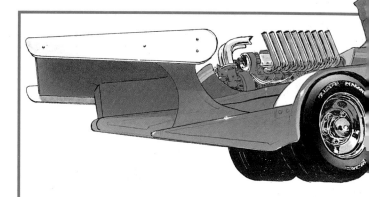

Racing cars and their teams are transported to and from racetracks in giant trailers (below). They house the car, a workshop compartment and living quarters for the team – a kitchen, lounge and shower, sometimes a bedroom too.

A super truck based on a Leyland Landtrain rears up into a wheelie (above).

Monster trucks like *BigFoot* (above) compete at truck meetings. They try to out do each other in events whilst doing wheelies and climbing over obstacles.

In the USA the NASCAR Craftsman Truck races draw large crowds. Below, a Craftsman Series super truck.

A clutch of 700 horsepower racing trucks make a dash for the first corner (right). Drivers say the latest racing trucks handle in a surprisingly similar way to racing cars. The main difference is that the truck bodies create less down-force to help them grip the track.

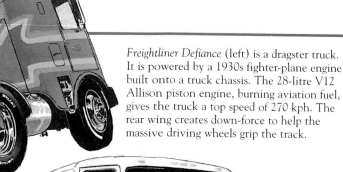

Freightliner Defiance (left) is a dragster truck. It is powered by a 1930s fighter-plane engine built onto a truck chassis. The 28-litre V12 Allison piston engine, burning aviation fuel, gives the truck a top speed of 270 kph. The rear wing creates down-force to help the massive driving wheels grip the track.

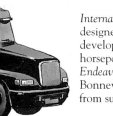

International Endeavour III (above) is a unique truck designed to set speed records. Its diesel engine develops 2,500 horsepower, compared to less than 500 horsepower for a normal road truck. *International Endeavour III* has reached a speed of 360 kph on the Bonneville Salt Flats in Utah, USA. To slow down from such a high speed, it has to use parachutes.

Construction Trucks

The construction industry depends on heavy trucks to move enormous quantities of materials to and from construction sites. Whatever the type of structure being built, from homes or skyscrapers to roads or bridges, large volumes of concrete are always needed, so concrete-mixer trucks are frequent visitors to construction sites. Vehicles that spend most of their time on rough or loose ground are sometimes fitted with low-pressure tyres that hug the ground better for improved grip. Dump trucks are often used to move materials around construction sites. These small trucks have a large bucket for carrying materials and are very manoeuvrable. Some of them are jointed in the middle so they can turn into the tightest of spaces.

Road crane

A truck chassis can have a range of bodies and machinery built on it. One specialised type of truck is the road crane. The crane is made from a series of sections that slide inside each other for easy transport. There is one cab for driving the vehicle and another for operating the crane.

Articulated Trucks

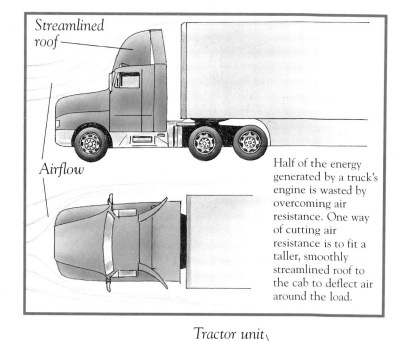

Streamlined roof

Airflow

Half of the energy generated by a truck's engine is wasted by overcoming air resistance. One way of cutting air resistance is to fit a taller, smoothly streamlined roof to the cab to deflect air around the load.

The largest trucks are articulated, which means that they have a swivel joint behind the driver's cab. The joint lets the truck manoeuvre more easily than a rigid truck of the same size. The rear part of the truck, where the freight is carried, can also be disconnected and replaced within minutes by a different load. The back of the truck is called a semi-trailer, because it has no road-wheels at the front. The front of the semi-trailer rests on the back of the tractor unit. When a semi-trailer has to be unhitched from its tractor, small temporary wheels are lowered to hold it up.

Tractor unit

Semi-trailer

Air filter

In-line layout

Hinged hood

Exhaust pipe

The in-line layout truck design is most popular in the USA, where there is more room on the highways for the long-nose models. The biggest advantage of the in-line layout (above and below) is that the engine is easy to get to for repairs and servicing. The whole engine cover, or hood, hinges up and forward (above). To save weight, the hood is often made from fibreglass, which is lighter than metal, but just as strong. US trucks often gleam with polished chrome-work. The tall vertical exhaust pipes, drum-shaped air filter and radiator grille at the front are often finished in chrome.

Radiator grille

Engine hood

Trunnion plate

The link between an articulated truck's tractor and semi-trailer is called the fifth wheel. A tractor is hitched up to a semi-trailer by reversing up to it. The semi-trailer rides up onto a plate called a trunnion plate, fitted to the back of the tractor (above). As the tractor continues reversing, a pin pointing down from the front of the semi-trailer drops into a hole in the middle of the plate, linking the two parts of the vehicle together. Finally, the semi-trailer's temporary front wheels are raised.

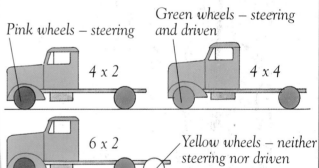

Pink wheels – steering

Green wheels – steering and driven

4 x 2

4 x 4

6 x 2

Yellow wheels – neither steering nor driven

6 x 4

6 x 6

Most family cars have two axles with a wheel on each end. One of the axles is driven (or controlled) by the engine. Trucks have more axles, and more than one of them may be driven. A truck with two axles, one driven, is described as a 4 x 2 which means it has four wheels, two of which are driven.

8 x 4

Tippers and Lifters

Tipper trucks and dump trucks carry heavy loads of loose material which they unload by tipping up the back of the truck. Tippers transport their loads by road while dumpers move materials about within construction sites. The back of the truck is raised by one or more hydraulic rams. A hydraulic ram is a piston that is forced through a tube by oil pressure, powered by the truck's engine. Longer rams are made from several pistons that slide inside each other. Hydraulic rams are also the mechanical muscles that power a variety of other lifting devices used by trucks.

Skip truck

Hydraulic arm

Skip

A skip truck (above) has two hydraulic arms at the back for loading and unloading skips – metal containers for transporting rubbish and other materials.

Forklift truck

This modern version of the traditional forklift truck (above) can raise and lower a load like a normal forklift, and it can also reach its arm forwards to place loads onto shelves.

The Terex Titan (below) is the world's biggest dumper truck. It works at mines and quarries, where it can transport up to 550 tonnes of rubble or mineral ore at a time.

*1927 Autocar
tipper truck*

Dustbin lorry

Levers powered
by the engine

The tipping mechanism of early
tipper trucks, like the 1927 Autocar
model (above), were operated by
levers powered by the vehicle's small
20 or 30 horsepower engine. A
modern tipper (below) is raised by a
hydraulic ram that can call on an
engine of 200-500 horsepower,
sometimes more, to tip greater loads.
The cabs of works trucks like tippers
are basic compared to the cabs of
long-distance trucks.

Hopper

(above)
tor to
d rubbish
space. The
ed into an
t the back
ight).
pper is full,
r is used. A
anel swings
bbish,
scoops it
he truck.

Hydraulic ram

Hopper

Rubbish

Compactor

1

2

3

4

The hopper is filled
with rubbish (1). The
compactor swings out
over the rubbish (2)
moves down behind
it and crushes it (3)
and scoops it out of
the hopper into the
truck (4).

Military Trucks

World War I truck

Military trucks are essential for transporting soldiers and equipment. They have to be particularly rugged and reliable, as well as easy to repair and maintain. Many military trucks are adapted from civilian models and strengthened especially for military service. Several different types of military vehicle can be built from the same basic chassis. One model might be a general transport truck, another might be a fuel tanker and another might have a crane on the back. In addition to general transport work, military trucks also have to carry troops, tow equipment and sometimes carry weapons. All-terrain models have a high ground clearance (the space under the truck) to protect the under-side of the vehicle from damage on rough ground. Trucks intended to operate in combat zones have to be armour-plated for extra protection.

Military trucks such as the one above were used in large numbers for the first time during World War I (1914-18). They frequently broke down and their thin wheels sank into the mud, but they still managed to prove their usefulness as military transporters.

The six-wheel General Motors GMC CCKW 353 (right) is one of the best known American military trucks. More than half a million of them were made after 1941. It was a rugged and reliable truck that remained in service for decades.

GMC CCKW 353

Tank transporter　　*Battletank*

Battletanks are transported by road on tank transporters (above). These powerful vehicles spread the immense weight of a tank (30-65 tonnes) over a greater area to prevent damage to the road surface. They also burn less fuel than the tank and move faster.

An army road-crane, the military version of the Swedish Scania P113 HK, rescues a vehicle that has run into trouble (right). In addition to the crane it has a winch. All three of the truck's axles are driven by the vehicle's 11-litre, 380 horsepower engine to give better grip. The engine is modular, meaning that it is built from a simple set of parts that are easy to replace if a repair is needed. The ring on the roof of the cab is for mounting a machine-gun.

An AM General M923 five-tonne truck (right) tows a howitzer (a type of gun). This truck lets the driver alter the tyre pressure from inside the cab. Lowering the pressure makes the tyres softer and better able to grip soft ground.

AM General M923

Howitzer

Military breakdown crane

Caterpillar tracks

Machine gun mount

Scania P113 HK

SCANIA

113 H   310

65416

A military crane lifts out a tank's engine and lowers a replacement into position (above). The crane is fitted with caterpillar tracks instead of wheels, to stop it sinking into soft ground. Each track is an endless chain of links that spread the vehicle's weight.

23

Fire Engines

Modern fire engines can be traced back to the first fire engines built in Britain in the 17th century. These early machines were simply hand-operated water-pumps mounted on wheels. Modern fire engines are much more advanced multi-function vehicles. More complex than ordinary trucks, they carry fire-fighters into action and provide pumping power for water-jets and other equipment such as hydraulic ladders and elevator platforms. They also carry the equipment necessary to fight fires and also to tackle a variety of rescue operations. If extra equipment is needed, it can be brought to the scene by emergency trucks called rescue tenders.

This 1903 Merryweather Fire King (above) was driven by a steam engine, which also powered the water pump. It could pump about 1,800 litres of water every minute.

Merryweather made some of the earliest fire engines in Britain to have petrol engines. This 1903 model with a hose reel and wheeled escape ladder served in London (below).

Water hydrant

24

Remote cities like Darwin, on Australia's north coast, depend on deliveries of freight by road train from ports like Sydney, in the south.

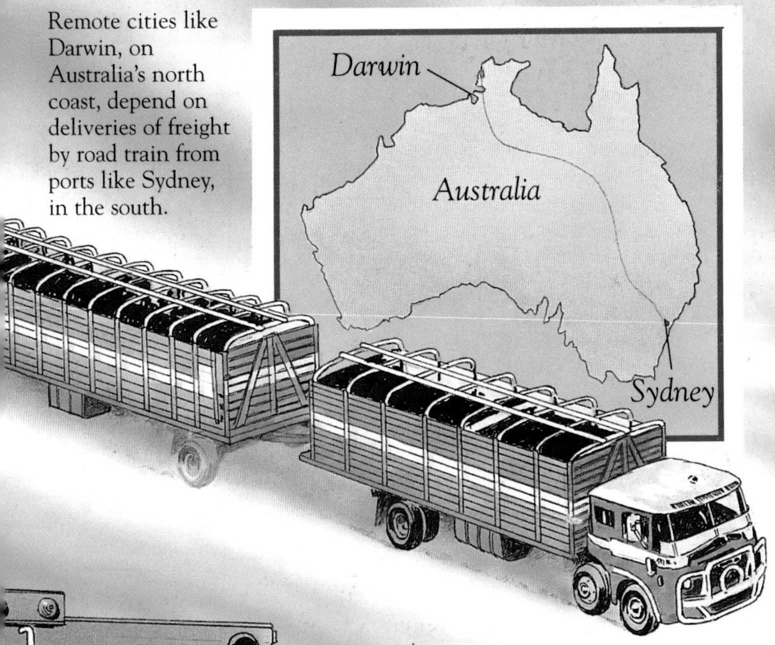

Darwin

Australia

Sydney

Monitor

6 26

2

Major airports worldwide have their own fire and rescue services (above). Since airport fires may involve aviation fuel, airport fire trucks spray foam instead of water from directional nozzles called monitors on top of the trucks.

A hydraulic ladder (right) is mounted on a rotating base or turntable, so that it can be turned and raised in any direction.

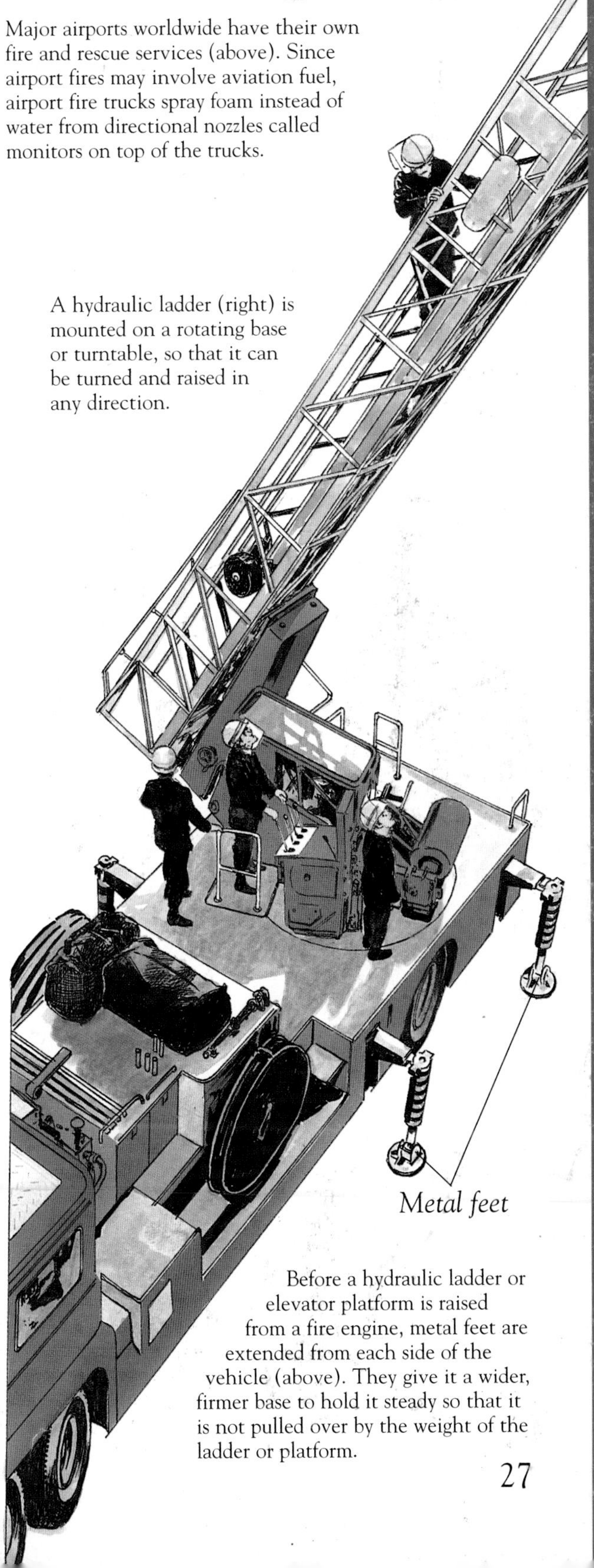

Roo bars

TRAIN

Metal feet

Before a hydraulic ladder or elevator platform is raised from a fire engine, metal feet are extended from each side of the vehicle (above). They give it a wider, firmer base to hold it steady so that it is not pulled over by the weight of the ladder or platform.

27

Trucks to Come

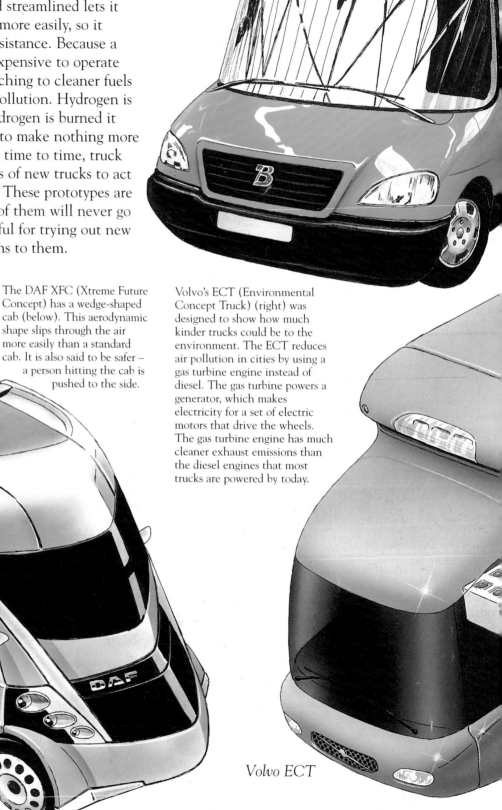

Prototype for multi-drop delivery truck

Designs for future trucks are being shaped by two main factors – the need to cut costs and reduce air pollution. Making a truck more slick and streamlined lets it slip through the air more easily, so it wastes less fuel overcoming air resistance. Because a vehicle burns less fuel, it is less expensive to operate and it reduces air pollution. Switching to cleaner fuels is an even better way to reduce pollution. Hydrogen is the cleanest fuel of all. When hydrogen is burned it combines with oxygen in the air to make nothing more harmful than water vapour. From time to time, truck manufacturers produce prototypes of new trucks to act as showcases for new technology. These prototypes are also called concept trucks. Most of them will never go into production, but they are useful for trying out new ideas and testing people's reactions to them.

The DAF XFC (Xtreme Future Concept) has a wedge-shaped cab (below). This aerodynamic shape slips through the air more easily than a standard cab. It is also said to be safer – a person hitting the cab is pushed to the side.

Volvo's ECT (Environmental Concept Truck) (right) was designed to show how much kinder trucks could be to the environment. The ECT reduces air pollution in cities by using a gas turbine engine instead of diesel. The gas turbine powers a generator, which makes electricity for a set of electric motors that drive the wheels. The gas turbine engine has much cleaner exhaust emissions than the diesel engines that most trucks are powered by today.

DAF XFC

Volvo ECT

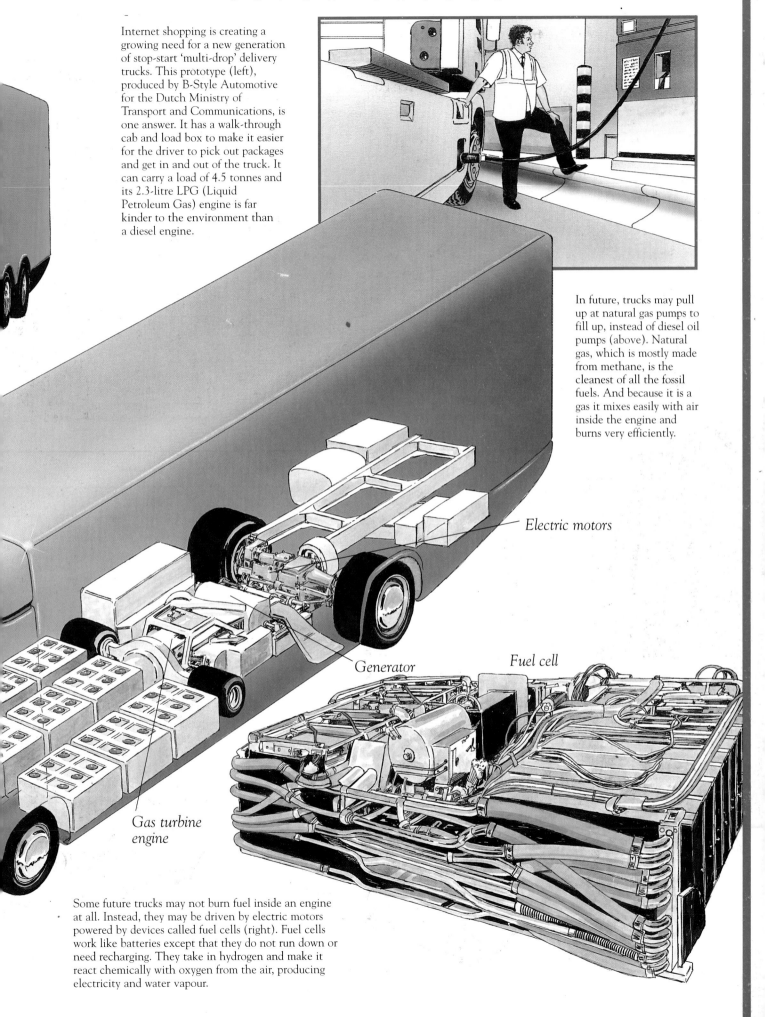

Internet shopping is creating a growing need for a new generation of stop-start 'multi-drop' delivery trucks. This prototype (left), produced by B-Style Automotive for the Dutch Ministry of Transport and Communications, is one answer. It has a walk-through cab and load box to make it easier for the driver to pick out packages and get in and out of the truck. It can carry a load of 4.5 tonnes and its 2.3-litre LPG (Liquid Petroleum Gas) engine is far kinder to the environment than a diesel engine.

In future, trucks may pull up at natural gas pumps to fill up, instead of diesel oil pumps (above). Natural gas, which is mostly made from methane, is the cleanest of all the fossil fuels. And because it is a gas it mixes easily with air inside the engine and burns very efficiently.

Electric motors

Generator

Fuel cell

Gas turbine engine

Some future trucks may not burn fuel inside an engine at all. Instead, they may be driven by electric motors powered by devices called fuel cells (right). Fuel cells work like batteries except that they do not run down or need recharging. They take in hydrogen and make it react chemically with oxygen from the air, producing electricity and water vapour.

Glossary

Aerodynamic
Able to move easily through air.

Aviation fuel
Fuel used to power aeroplanes.

Axle
A rod that passes through the centre of a wheel.

Caterpillar tracks
A series of metal plates linked together and fitted over a vehicle's wheels.

Chrome-work
Parts of a vehicle coated with chromium, a silver-coated metal.

Cylinder
One of the metal tubes inside an engine, where the fuel is burned.

Diesel
A type of engine, invented by the German engineer Rudolf Diesel.

Dragster
A powerful racing vehicle designed to accelerate as fast as possible down a track 400 m long.

Fibreglass
A material made from woven glass fibres embedded in plastic.

Fossil fuels
Natural fuels such as coal and gas which were formed millions of years ago from the remains of living organisms.

Freight
The goods carried by different forms of transport.

Gas turbine engine
A type of engine that burns fuel to produce gas, which spins a turbine (a finned wheel which is turned as gas rushes past it and pushes against the fins).

Haulage industry
An industry which makes money from the transport of goods.

Hoist
A lifting device or machine.

Horsepower
A measure of how fast an engine converts the energy in its fuel into movement energy.

Hydrant
A pipe in the street which is attached to the main water supply so that water can be drawn from it with a hosepipe.

Hydraulic
Operated by pressurised fluid.

Hydrogen
A colourless, odourless and tasteless gas.

Locomotives
Engines which pull railway carriages and freight wagons.

Pneumatic
Air-filled.

Prototype
The first, or original, model of a vehicle used to test its design before it goes into production.

Tractor
A vehicle used to pull heavy loads, such as the cab and engine units that pull articulated trucks.

Winch
A motor-driven drum used to lift things by winding rope or cable around the drum.

Super Truck Facts

The biggest transport vehicles ever built are the two crawler transporters that carried the Apollo/Saturn 5 moon-landing rockets to the launch pad in the 1960s and 1970s. They are now used to carry the Space Shuttle and its mobile launch platform to the launch pad.

Tyres for the world's biggest dumper trucks can weigh up to 5.6 tonnes each and stand more than 3.5 m high.

Trucks can have up to 18 forward gears and two reverse gears, compared to five forward gears and one reverse for a family car.

Truck drivers spend so much time at the wheel that their seats have their own suspension systems to make them more comfortable to sit in for long periods.

On long journeys, a truck driver may have to be away from home overnight. Some cabs are fitted with bunks to sleep in and even a refrigerator, coffee machine and microwave oven for preparing meals.

The latest trucks have on-board computers that keep the driver fully informed about the state of the truck's engine. If a fault develops, the on-board computer can give details of what has gone wrong.

Truck drivers can be connected to their base by satellite radio. This means that the truck's position can be pinpointed at any time.

The longest truck in the world is 174 m long and is called Le Tourneau Arctic Snow Train. It was built for the US army to use in arctic regions.

Amphibious trucks are able to drive both across land and through water.

It is quite usual for a truck driver to cover about 160,000 km in a year.

During World War I (1914-1918) the number of transport vehicles near the front line in France increased from 6,000 to 92,000.

Chronology

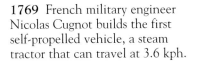

1769 French military engineer Nicolas Cugnot builds the first self-propelled vehicle, a steam tractor that can travel at 3.6 kph.

1784 Scotsman William Murdock builds a working model of a steam-powered carriage.

1789 Oliver Evans is granted the first American patent for a steam-powered land vehicle.

1801 English engineer Richard Trevithick builds a steam-powered carriage.

1815 Scottish engineer John McAdam invents a new road surface called tarmacadam made from crushed rock and tar.

1831 A steam-powered ten-seat bus starts a passenger service between London and Stratford.

1845 Scotsman Robert William Thomson invents the rubber tyre.

1858 The first successful steam-powered fire engine is introduced.

1863 Jean-Joseph-Etienne Lenoir builds the first vehicle powered by an internal combustion engine instead of a steam engine.

1885 Karl Benz builds a three-wheel automobile powered by an internal combustion engine that burns gasoline fuel.

1887 Gottlieb Daimler builds a four-wheel automobile powered by an internal combustion engine.

1888 Scotsman John Boyd Dunlop invents the pneumatic (air-filled) rubber tyre.

1891 The French engineers Andre and Edouard Michelin invent an inflatable tyre that can be removed from the wheel rim and replaced by another tyre.

1892 French engineer Rudolf Diesel invents a new type of engine, the diesel engine, that will later power trucks and other commercial vehicles.

1895 The Benz company builds a petrol fuelled bus.

1902 Drum brakes and disc brakes, the two types of brakes used by modern trucks, are invented.

1903 The first petrol-fuelled fire engine is introduced.

1908 The first twin wheels for trucks are introduced. A twin wheel is two wheels on the same axle where there was only one before.

1913 The removable steel wheel is introduced. Trucks begin to carry spare wheels.

1914 An American automobile repair man, Ernest Holmes, designs the world's first wrecker truck.

1915 Detroit blacksmith August Fruehauf invents the tractor trailer, a truck with a separate driver's cab and trailer.

1916 4,500 trucks, buses and ambulances help to transport four million French troops to defend Verdun in France, during World War I.

1917 The French army uses a specially built fleet of trucks to transport carrier pigeons. Each truck holds 80 birds in 19 cages. The birds are used to carry messages tied to their legs.

1921 The first motorway is built, in Germany.

1925 The Michelin company develops a low-pressure heavy goods vehicle tyre.

1930 English engineer Bernard Dicksee builds a diesel engine that can be used by road vehicles. The 8.1-litre, six-cylinder engine is fitted in trucks.

1939 The first vehicles with automatic clutches, to make gear changing faster and easier, are introduced.

1941 The first Jeep, a general purpose military vehicle, is introduced.

1947 The Goodyear company introduces the tubeless tyre.

1951 Power steering is introduced by Chrysler.

1954 The size of containers, used for transporting freight on trucks, is standardised.

1982 The first truck diesel emission regulations come into force in Britain.

1983 The gross weight of trucks allowed by law on British roads is increased from 32 tonnes to 38 tonnes.

1996 Ron Hornaday wins his second US NASCAR Craftsman Truck Series championship.

1997 A dragster truck called *Joint Venture*, based on a Freightliner FLD120 truck, sets a speed record of 362.9 kph on the Bonneville Salt Flats in Utah, USA.

1998 Ron Hornaday wins his second US NASCAR Craftsman Truck Series championship.

1999 Jack Sprague wins the US NASCAR Craftsman Truck Series championship for the second time.

Index